MAKING BOOKS

Gillian Chapman and Pam Robson

SIMON & SCHUSTER
YOUNG BOOKS

To all the children who shared their books with us and gave us inspiration. We hope our book will achieve as much.

G.C. and P.R.

We had to do some pages twice because the circles had wobbly edges ..... but the worst was when it got dirty. Shehara.

Finishing a book is like something you can't explain It is a very nice feeling and I want to make a book again. Mark.

It is hard work to make a book. You have to think of who it is for and whether they will understand it. Julie

I helped make a book, I hope you stopped to take a look. Lisa.

I'm really proud of our book. Lisa W.

I had never made a book before. It was difficult to make but it was fun. Jyoti

Design and book making: Gillian Chapman

Commissioning editor: Daphne Butler
Typography: Brigitte Willgoss
Photography: Rupert Horrox

First published in Great Britain in 1991
by Simon & Schuster Young Books

Reprinted 1993

Simon & Schuster Young Books
Wolsey House, Wolsey Road
Hemel Hempstead, Herts HP2 4SS

Printed and bound in Belgium by
Proost International Book Production

Text copyright © Gillian Chapman and Pam Robson 1991
Illustration copyright © Gillian Chapman 1991

British Library Cataloguing in Publication Data
Chapman, Gillian
  Making books.
  1. Books. Making
  I. Title   II. Robson, Pam
  686

ISBN 0–7500–0840–7

CONTENTS

bookmarks

Making a Book is a Lot of Fun!
Anyone can make a book–it is a
thrilling way to share your ideas.
Look at all the different books on
these pages. There are lots of
unusual designs to choose from.
Each book has a special character
of its own. Notice the exciting
variety of shapes and colours, the
lovely selection of papers and
textures. The ideas in **Making
Books** will help you make *your*
book unique.

Books can inform and entertain
us. They can tell us stories. Think
carefully about those who are going
to read your book. You may want to
make a book full of surprises and
pop-ups–you may want to make
one that is full of interesting facts.

moving whe
▲ book

mix and mat
▼ book

collage book
(paper) ▼

shaped
book
▼

stepped
book ◄

4

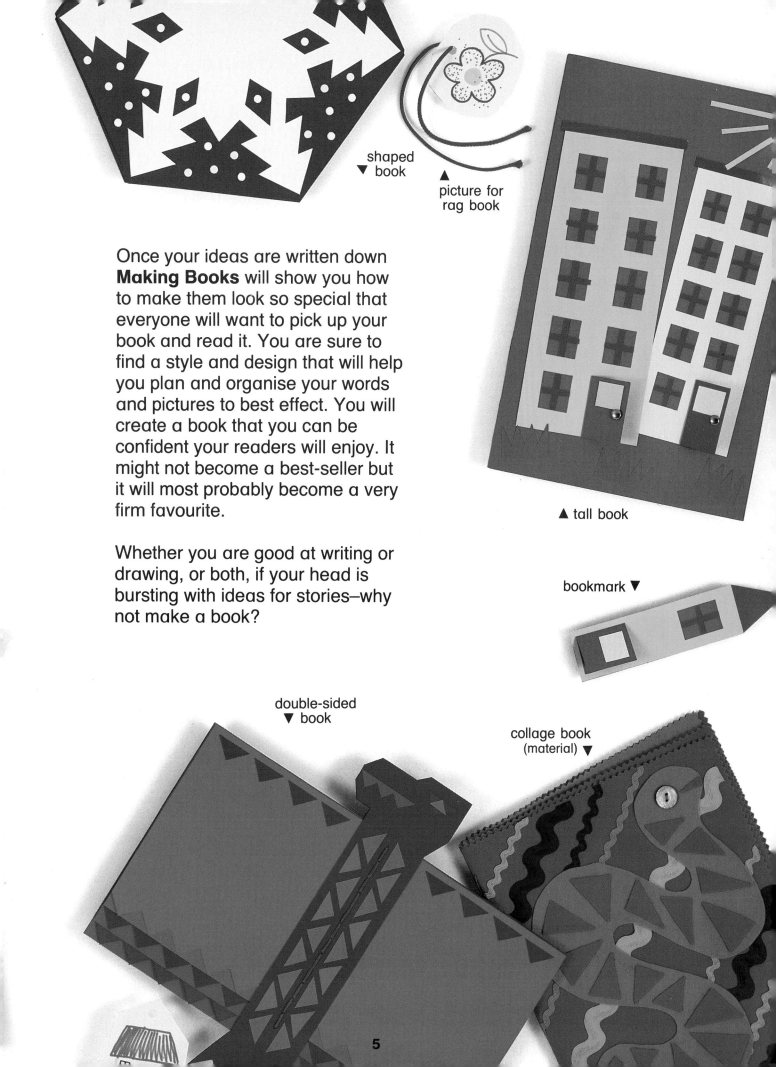

shaped
▼ book

▲
picture for
rag book

Once your ideas are written down **Making Books** will show you how to make them look so special that everyone will want to pick up your book and read it. You are sure to find a style and design that will help you plan and organise your words and pictures to best effect. You will create a book that you can be confident your readers will enjoy. It might not become a best-seller but it will most probably become a very firm favourite.

Whether you are good at writing or drawing, or both, if your head is bursting with ideas for stories—why not make a book?

▲ tall book

bookmark ▼

double-sided
▼ book

collage book
(material) ▼

5

When short of time, you may need to know how to make a book quickly. Although you may not have much time to spend on the design, it is still worth thinking carefully about basic details.

Choosing the Paper
Choose a colour for the paper that will match the contents. You might even decide to use a different colour for each page. If you use white paper or card, you can write or draw straight on to the pages.

Making a Simple Booklet
By folding the sheets of paper together, you can make a book very quickly. It is best to lie the book open and staple along the centre fold with a long-arm stapler. The pictures and writing can then be glued-in 'scrapbook' style. If you staple along the spine with the book closed, it may not stay open when you want it to.

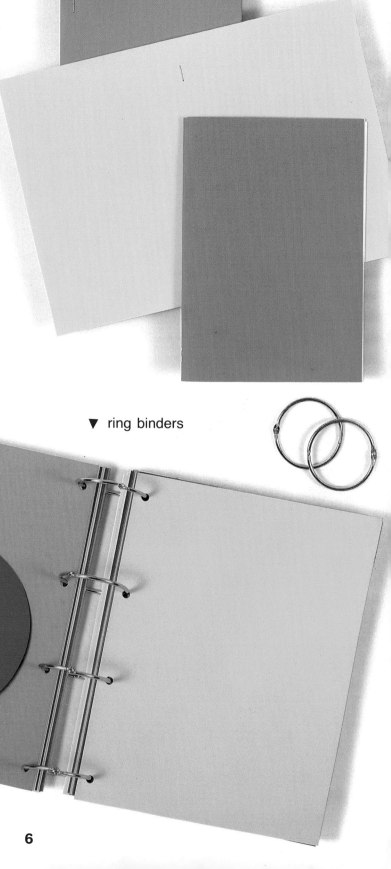

◀ don't staple down fold

staple along
▶ centre fold

▼ ring binders

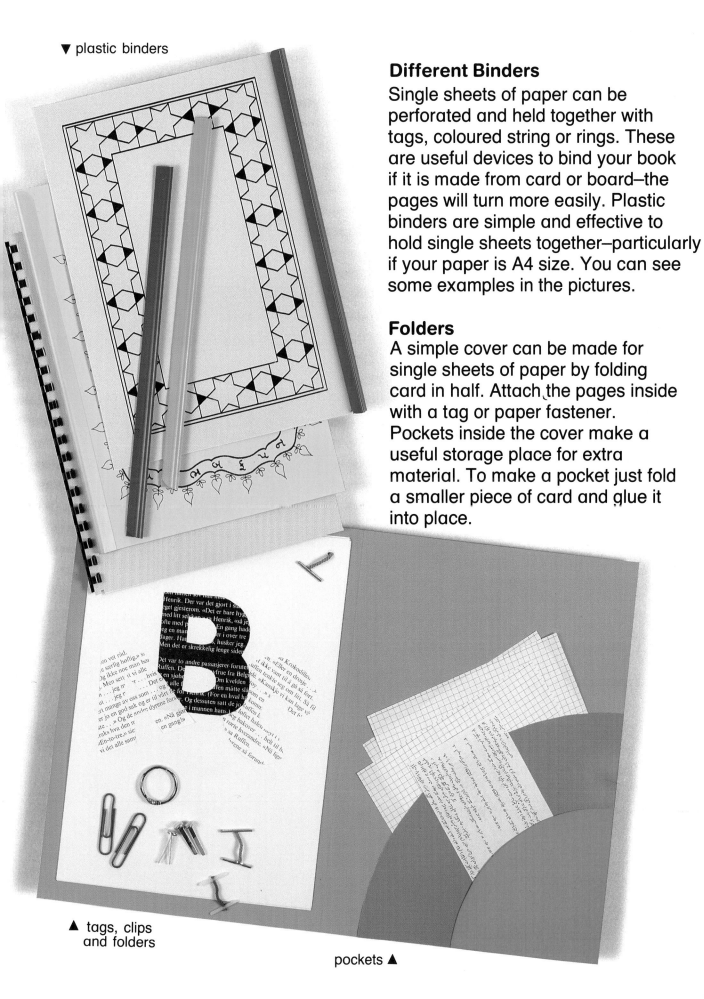

▼ plastic binders

Different Binders

Single sheets of paper can be perforated and held together with tags, coloured string or rings. These are useful devices to bind your book if it is made from card or board—the pages will turn more easily. Plastic binders are simple and effective to hold single sheets together—particularly if your paper is A4 size. You can see some examples in the pictures.

Folders

A simple cover can be made for single sheets of paper by folding card in half. Attach the pages inside with a tag or paper fastener. Pockets inside the cover make a useful storage place for extra material. To make a pocket just fold a smaller piece of card and glue it into place.

▲ tags, clips and folders

pockets ▲

Scrap material can be used to make rag books for very small children. If bright colours are chosen, you can make a book which is both attractive and strong.

Making the Pages
Make a paper pattern the size of the open book. Pin the pattern on to the material and cut round it—this way you will be sure that all the pages are exactly the same size. Lie the material pages on top of each other. Join them together by sewing along the centre.

Attaching the Pictures
Tie drawings or photographs into your book with laces or coloured pieces of wool or string. If they are covered with self-adhesive plastic first, they will last longer. Punch a hole in each picture to thread the fastening through. Words can be written with fabric markers.

◀ material   ▲ centre fold   ▲ paper pattern

▶ rag book

my book by Farina

tie your pictures into your book
▼

8

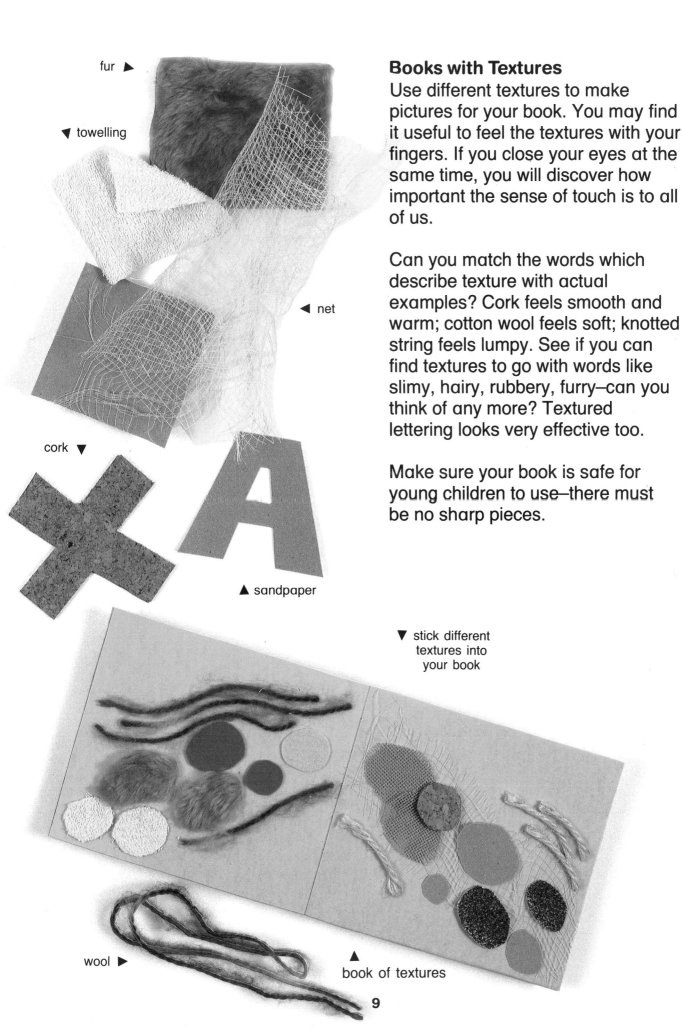

fur ▶

◀ towelling

◀ net

cork ▼

▲ sandpaper

Books with Textures

Use different textures to make pictures for your book. You may find it useful to feel the textures with your fingers. If you close your eyes at the same time, you will discover how important the sense of touch is to all of us.

Can you match the words which describe texture with actual examples? Cork feels smooth and warm; cotton wool feels soft; knotted string feels lumpy. See if you can find textures to go with words like slimy, hairy, rubbery, furry—can you think of any more? Textured lettering looks very effective too.

Make sure your book is safe for young children to use—there must be no sharp pieces.

▼ stick different
textures into
your book

wool ▶

▲
book of textures

9

Japanese Paper Zig-Zag Book

Some Japanese books are made from long lengths of folded paper with neither sewing nor stapling. The pages can be turned as in an ordinary book or the book can be unfolded. To make a zig-zag book in the Japanese style fold a long strip of paper several times. The paper can be as long as you wish. By attaching strong card to either end you can strengthen your book. Your pictures and writing can be on one or both sides.

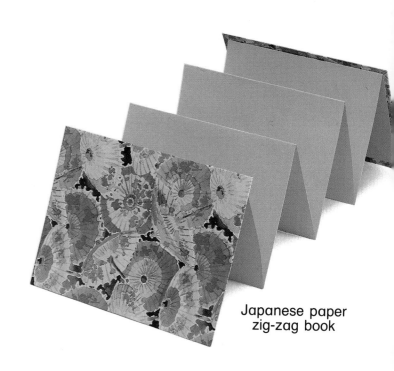

Japanese paper
zig-zag book

Making a Strong Zig-Zag Book

1. Line up two pieces of card, leaving a gap of 2 cm between them as shown below.

2. Cut lengths of tape 6 cm longer than the card. Join the two pieces of card with the tape, folding the excess tape over at the ends.

3. Cut a piece of tape the same length as the pages and cover the gap between the pages.

Free-Standing Zig-Zag Book

Sometimes a book may have no real beginning or end. If you have made a zig-zag book, you can join the two ends to make a story in the round. A book of animals will look like an animal carousel. A real-life story in the round is the life-cycle of the butterfly. You can see it in the picture opposite.

▼ join with tape

add
▼ facing tape

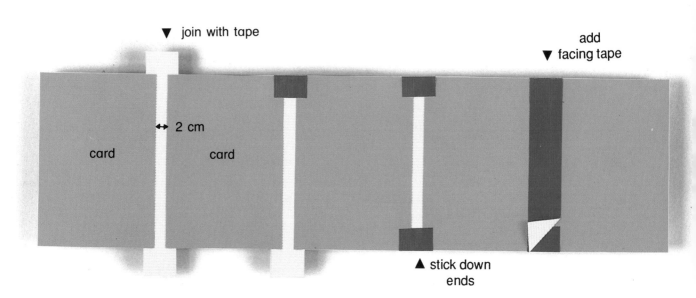

↔ 2 cm

card

card

▲ stick down
ends

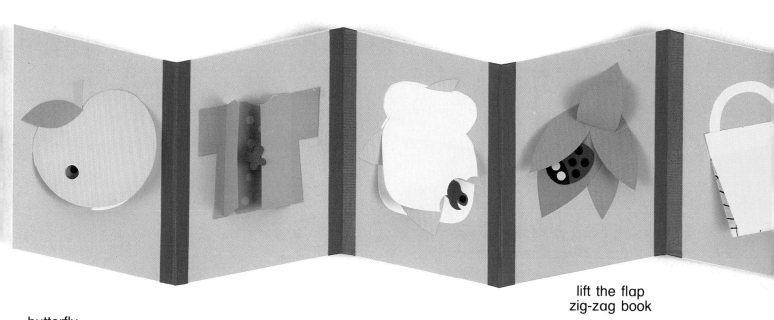

lift the flap
zig-zag book

butterfly
life cycle
zig-zag book

Other Ideas

To make your book hard-wearing, you can protect it by laminating each page. Your readers will have extra fun if you use velcro tabs or lift-the-flap devices like the ones shown here. Perhaps you could do your writing in two languages.

stick on ▼
numbers

matching numbers
zig-zag book

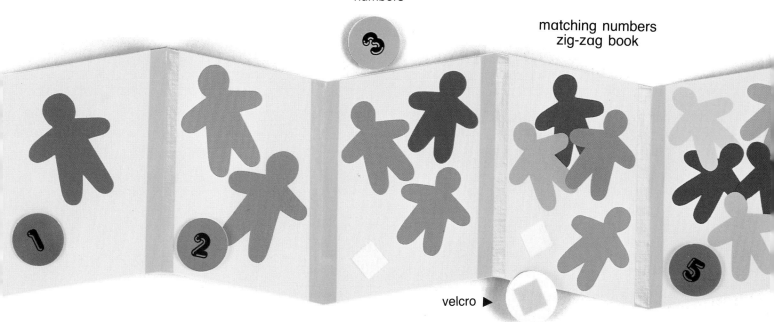

velcro ▶

Scrolls were used by many ancient cultures. The Old Testament written on a long parchment scroll is the focal point of the Jewish religious service. It is called the Torah.

Making a Scroll

To make a scroll just cut a length of paper to whatever size you need. Attach short pieces of wooden dowel to each end. These will prevent damage to your scroll.

Arrange your words and pictures as you would in an ordinary book. Remember to use only one side of the paper. You can decide whether to use the paper vertically or horizontally. It depends which will work best for you. Which way will be easiest to read? It helps if you divide the paper into pages by drawing lines across.

horizontal scroll ▼

▲ vertical scroll

Making a TV Book

By making a pretend TV set out of a cardboard box, you can turn a scroll into a TV book. You can mount the wooden dowels in the box so that they can be turned easily. If your scroll has pictures only, why not write a script to go with it? You could either read the script aloud or make a sound-track using a tape-recorder. If there is already text on your scroll you could add a musical sound-track.

cardboard ◄ box

cut window

cut holes ▲

scroll

wooden dowel ▶

▼ TV book

First the Hare ran fast....

soundtrack ◄ (try music or another language)

13

Sewing

A book which is sewn together will look professional and last longer. When you sew the pages of your book together, attach a strip of thin card to the centre fold. This will strengthen the spine.

Mark the centre fold using a pencil and ruler. Put dots where the sewing holes should be. The number of sewing holes will depend upon the size of your book, but it must be an *odd* number. Position them 2–3 cm apart. When the holes are marked first pierce them with a needle. Use a strong needle to sew the pages together. Follow the order of sewing shown in the diagram. Secure the ends tightly.

Binding

To make a really strong bound book with a spine, take two pieces of board and join them together with hessian. Cut a hessian strip 10 cm wide and 8 cm longer than the boards. The hessian must overlap the boards by 4 cm at the top and bottom, as shown here. Place the boards 2 cm apart. Glue the hessian to the boards.

Cover the boards with an attractive paper that you have chosen or designed. If you trim the corners of the paper, as shown in the picture, it will make the job of covering the book easier.

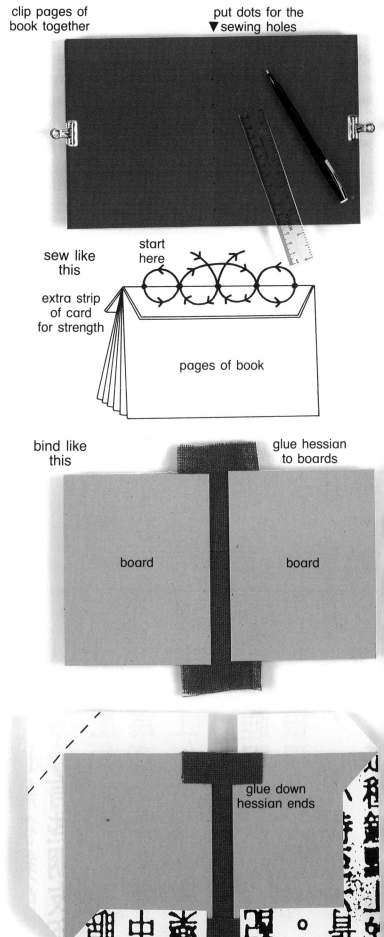

clip pages of book together

put dots for the ▼ sewing holes

sew like this

start here

extra strip of card for strength

pages of book

bind like this

glue hessian to boards

board

board

glue down hessian ends

cover outside of boards with attractive paper

Fixing the Pages

To fix the sewn pages inside the cover, first stick the strengthening card on to the hessian spine. Then glue the first and last pages down inside the front and back covers. These are called the **end papers**.

Leave the finished book beneath something heavy for a day before sticking any pictures or writing inside.

Bound books are very strong, like real books. They have the look and feel of real books that can be read over and over again.

strengthening card
sewn to spine

stick your
pictures and writing
to the pages

glue down the end
papers to the cover

15

SURPRISE PICTURES

With careful thought and planning you can make a book that is full of fun and surprises. By giving your book doors that open and flaps that lift, you can include lots of extra ideas that may not be written in the text. You could give the reader clues to solve or hidden objects to find. To do this you will have to work out the design of each page very carefully.

Double Books

These books have two sets of inside pages. You can see from the two examples here that they can be constructed very differently. One book has the spine down the centre; the other has two spines—one at each side of the book. If you are fortunate enough to be bilingual this is an opportunity to write a book using both of your languages.

Mix and Match

A mix and match book can make people laugh and is easy to make. Fasten or staple your pages of illustrations together along one side. Make one or two cuts through *all* the pages to divide the pictures into two or three parts. Do this carefully by measuring first. Do not cut right across the pages. For extra laughs use photographs of your friends or family.

mix and match book ▶

double books

Surprise Flaps

A surprise flap can be made if you want to hide objects on the pages of your book. Stick the flap down so that part of it can be lifted to reveal the surprise hiding underneath.

surprise flap
book

Surprise Windows and Doors

Cut around three of the sides of the windows and doors. Fold the fourth side so that it can be opened and closed. You may need to score the line of the fold first if the page is made from thin card. A paper fastener makes a good knob for a door–remember to cover the sharp ends. You will need a second sheet of paper behind these surprise windows and doors to draw the surprise picture on.

opening doors
▼ book

Moving Parts

You can make parts of your illustration move. Cut out separate pieces to go into the picture and fix them in place with paper fasteners. The story will come to life–wheels can turn, arms and legs can wave and kick, jaws can bite.

▲ moving wheels
book

◀ moving bodies book

Pop-up pictures give your book a third dimension. They can be challenging to make and are certainly exciting to see. A simple pop-up can be made by folding and cutting the page as shown below. This is a good idea if you want to make a mouth that opens and closes.

Push and Pull Flaps

The push and pull flap is also easy to make. Draw your picture on a strip of card and thread it through a slit in the page, as shown below.

Dinosaur Pop-Up

Choose where you want your dinosaur to pop-up and draw diagonal lines from corner to corner across the whole spread. Measure the distance between the point where the diagonal lines cross and the top of the page (distance x). Now make sure that your pop-up dinosaur is no taller than that distance. Allow an extra 1 cm strip along the bottom of the dinosaur. Fold the dinosaur in half vertically. Fold the 1 cm strip over and glue to the page along the diagonal lines.

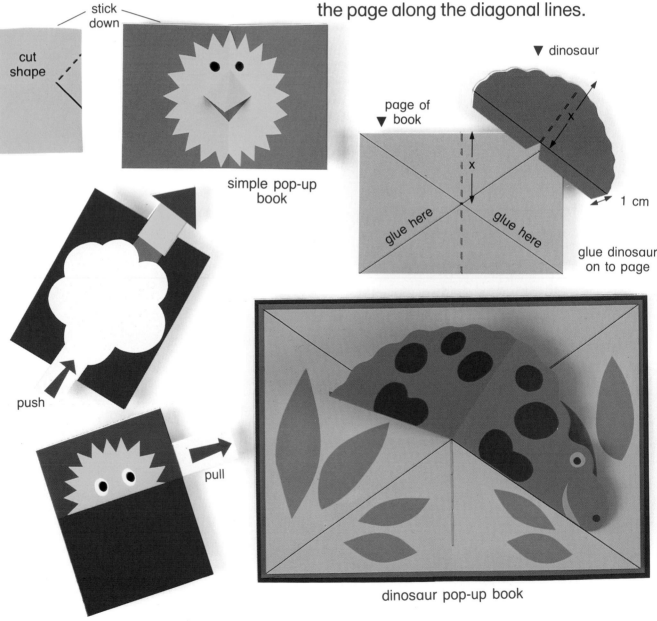

cut shape

stick down

simple pop-up book

push

pull

▼ dinosaur

page of ▼ book

x

x

glue here

glue here

1 cm

glue dinosaur on to page

dinosaur pop-up book

Tiger Pop-Up

To make a growling tiger cut a strip of thin card 3 cm wide and half the length of your double spread. Fold it in half. Fold each end over 1 cm and glue the ends. Lay the strip down the centre fold of your pages so that the creases match exactly. Stick the ends of the strip to the pages. Fold your pop-up tiger face in half and stick it on to the strip—matching up the creases. The tiger will now pop out when you open the page.

Monster Pop-Up

The monster pop-up needs 2 shapes (a and b). Fold the shapes in half and position them on the page. Leave enough for a 1 cm fold along the bottom edges. Be careful to check that all the creases match up and the pictures do not stick out of the page when the book is closed—then they can be stuck down. Cut arms, eyes, antennae, teeth and whiskers from scraps of paper or material and glue them to your pop-up. It can be transformed into a frog, a shark or a mad monster.

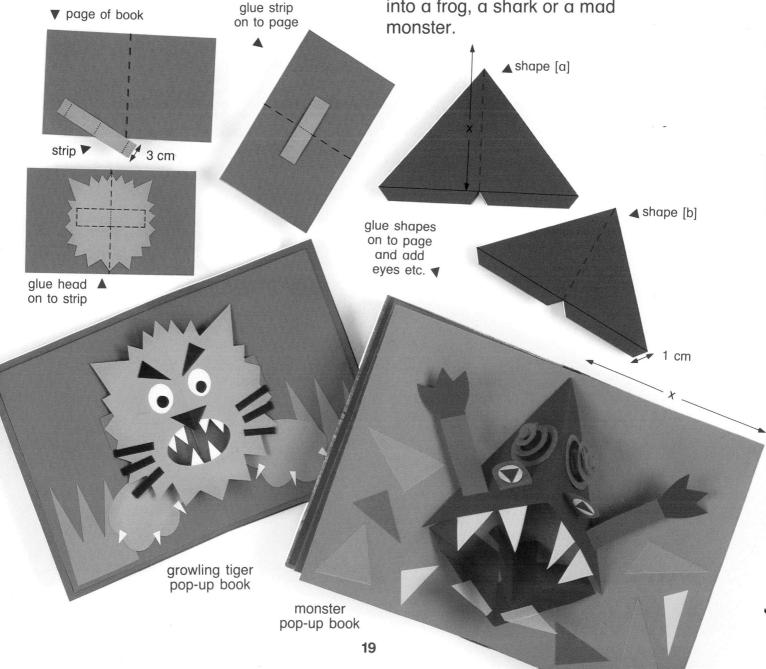

▼ page of book

glue strip on to page ▲

strip ▼   3 cm

glue head ▲ on to strip

▲ shape [a]

x

▲ shape [b]

glue shapes on to page and add eyes etc. ▼

1 cm

x

growling tiger pop-up book

monster pop-up book

Using Colour

Try to match the design with the contents. Think about the colour of the pages. Different colours create different moods. Yellow reminds us of sunshine, while red has a warm feeling too. Blue is a cold colour.

Choosing Sizes

At this planning stage think about the size of your book—the page size and the size of your lettering. These things will decide the **layout** of each page—how you arrange your writing and pictures.

Choosing the correct style and size of lettering is most important. A word processor is useful to try out different styles of lettering.

Each page will need careful planning. You don't want blank pages at the end or writing squashed into the last page because you have run out of pages. By drawing up a **page-plan** you can see the layout of the whole book at a glance.

Your writing will probably need **editing** to make sure that you have the correct number of words for each page.

page plan

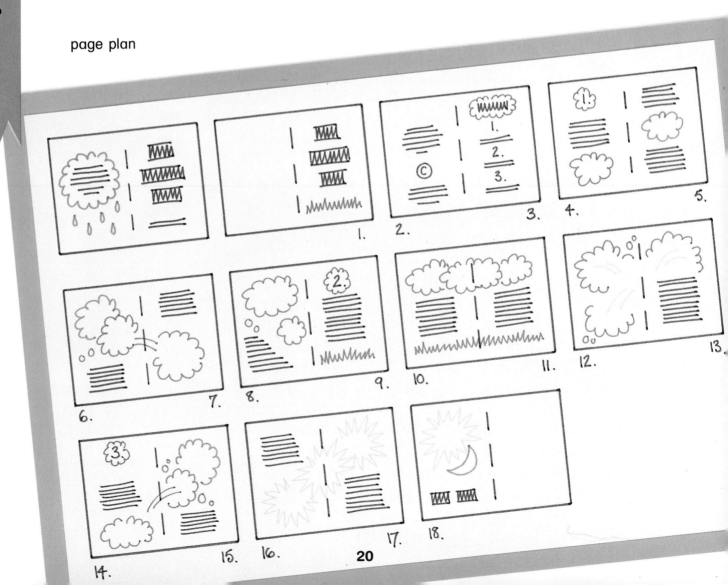

Arranging Words and Pictures

A **page-grid** will be helpful as a framework for each page. It will give you guidelines for positioning your pictures and writing. You will need the same page-grid for every page but this does not mean that every page must look alike. Look at the examples shown here.

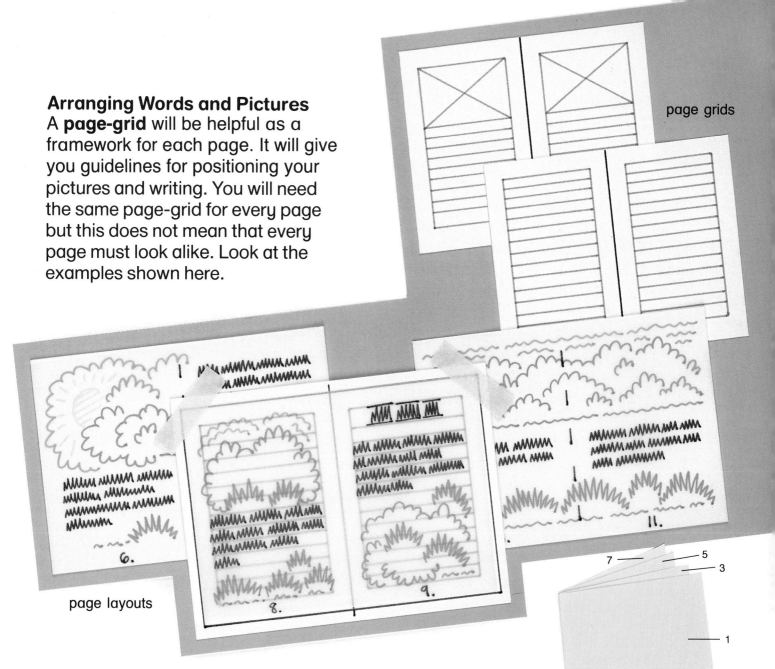

page grids

page layouts

It is best to keep your writing inside the lines of the page-grid but your pictures can flow over the lines. This will make your page design more interesting.

By placing tracing paper over the page-grid you can sketch in the finished layout to see how it looks.

Count with care the number of sheets of paper you need for your book. Remember you will be using both sides of each sheet.

Finishing Touches

Number the pages, include a **contents page**, and, if necessary, an **index**. You may even want to compile a **glossary**. Authors usually write credits naming people who have helped them.

You may want to dedicate your book to someone special.

BOOK SHAPES

It is very important to choose the right size and shape for your book. The size and shape is known as the **format**.

Basic Shapes
There are two basic formats to choose from. A tall format is called **portrait** and would be suitable for stories about space rockets or trees which need tall pictures that fill the tall shape of the pages. A wide format is called **landscape** and would be suitable for stories about train journeys, rivers or wriggling caterpillars which need long pictures that flow along the length of the pages.

You can see how this idea works in the pictures below. The two books are about different homes. The row of houses suits the landscape format while the block of flats suits the portrait format.

Unusual Shapes
Your words and pictures may look best in a book that has an unusual format. Now the fun begins! Be careful with your ideas, if they are too complicated the reader will not be able to turn the pages easily, making it difficult to enjoy the book.

This is what designing your book is all about—you want it to look attractive but it must also work properly.

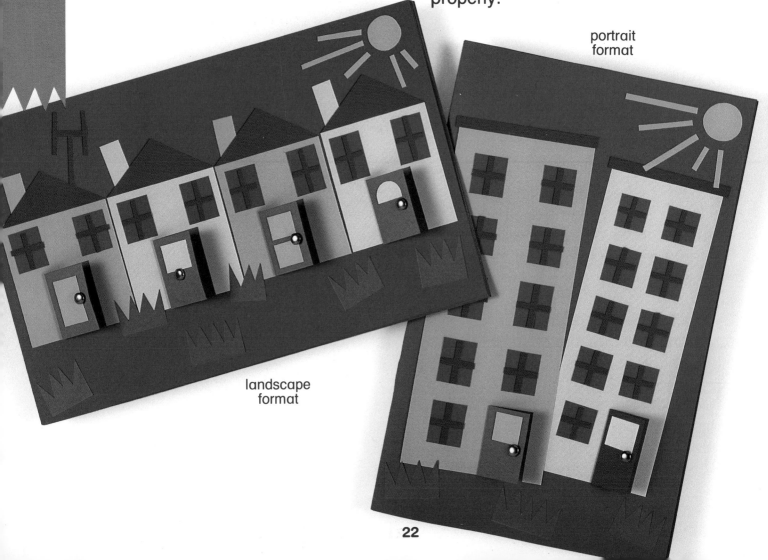

portrait
format

landscape
format

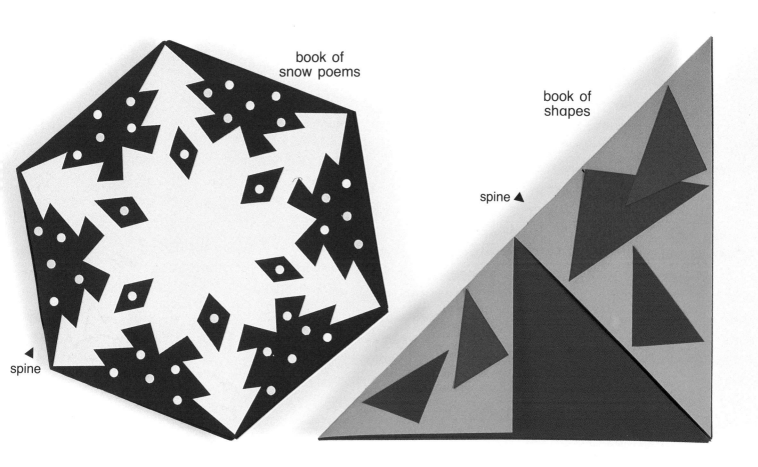

book of
snow poems

book of
shapes

spine ▲

◄ spine

book of
trees

Templates
Perhaps you and your friends are making books about the same topic. Why not first cut out one stiff shape from card? This is called a template. Everyone can draw round the template to make the book cover and the pages.

template for
fish book
▶

spine ▼

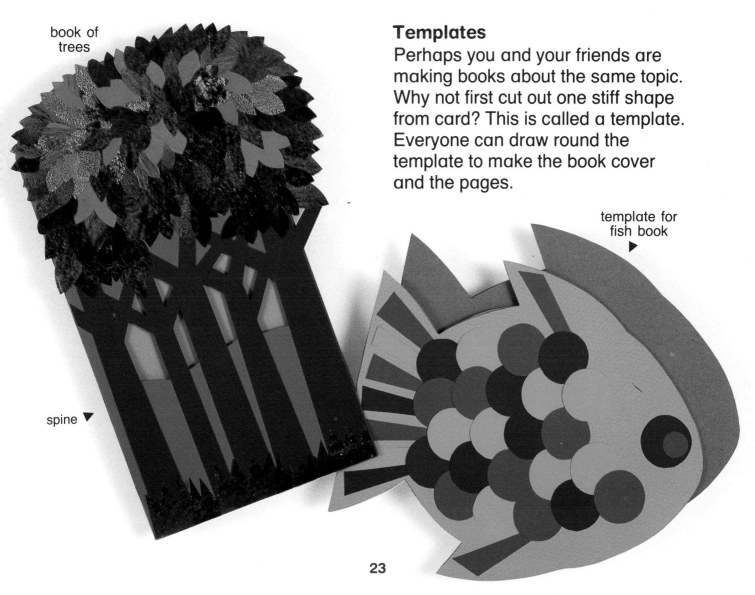

PRINTING

If you are not very good at drawing there are many colourful and effective ways to illustrate and decorate a book without having to draw any pictures!

The various printing techniques are an ideal way of repeating a theme or effect throughout a book.

Again, think carefully about the overall design of your book and decide how the different effects might best suit your text.

Patterned Borders
You might decide on a decorative border pattern around each page, using a simple printing block to make your pattern. Taken a step further, a border pattern can be photocopied and hand-coloured, ensuring that all the pages of the book will have a similar appearance.

printed borders

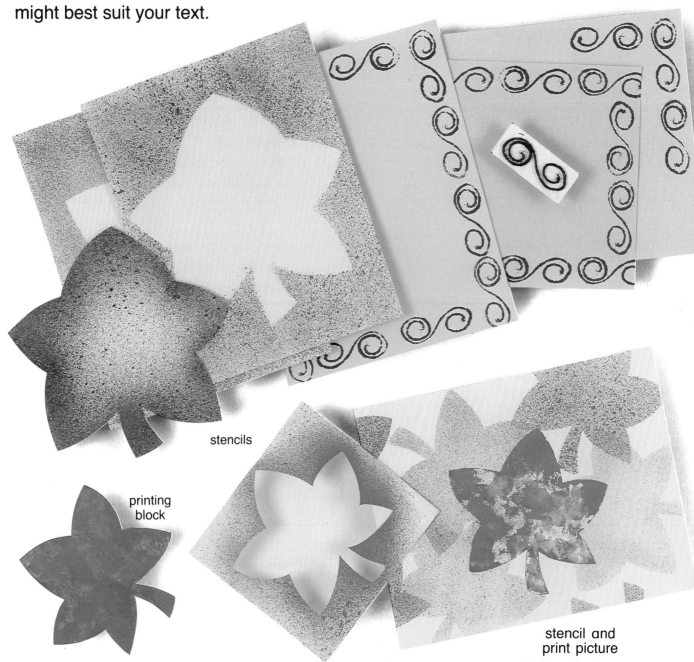

stencils

printing block

stencil and print picture

Using a Motif

A simple motif like a leaf shape could be repeated throughout a book in many forms. Use it as a splatter stencil for the inside pages, writing the text in the centre; use it as a simple card printing block, decorating the cover in multi-coloured prints; or take rubbings from real leaves using wax crayons, for a dramatic cover design.

Marbling

The use of marbled papers is traditional in book production. It gives a feeling of quality to a book. It is a technique which you can use to give your book a unique, distinctive appearance. Marbled papers can be used as end papers or on the cover.

wax rubbings

Use a deep plastic tray, larger than the paper you want to marble. Fill it with water. Add a few drops of vinegar and drop small amounts of oil-based paint on to the surface of the water. Mix the paint around, swirling the colours together until you achieve the effect you want.

Using a clean sheet of paper, place one edge on the surface of the water and slowly lower the whole sheet, making sure there are no air bubbles. Lift off carefully and leave your marbled paper to dry flat on some newspaper. Repeat the process until all the paint on the surface has gone. The marbling will become paler as you use up the paint.

marbled papers

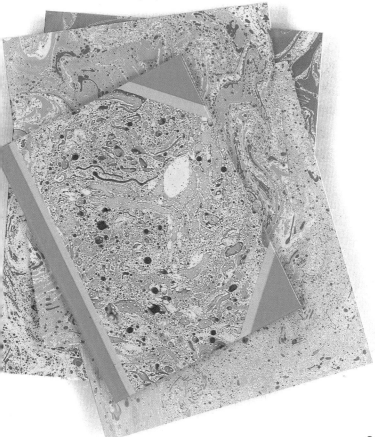

Collecting Materials

You need to collect various bits and pieces together and organise them into groups according to colour and texture. Coloured paper, pages from magazines, tissue paper, wrapping and packaging can all be used, as well as scraps of fabric, plastic, silver foil, felt, buttons, string and wool. Natural materials like feathers, dried flowers, grasses and leaves are effective but they can become a problem if they come unstuck!

Choosing Glues

The glues you decide to use will depend upon your materials. Papers are easy to stick down, but thicker materials may need stronger glue. Ask an adult for advice.

Special Effects

Natural forms, like leaves, can be protected and preserved by using a glaze. This can be made by diluting PVA glue with water. Cover your design with the glaze—it will dry shiny and protect your collage.

Covering bulkier collages with plastic film or silver foil can create interesting results, as well as offering protection. Painting over your collage using a metallic paint can also make a dramatic book cover.

A layered effect can be built up using the pages of your book with the collage on each page 'looking through' to the next page. Look at the underwater book opposite.

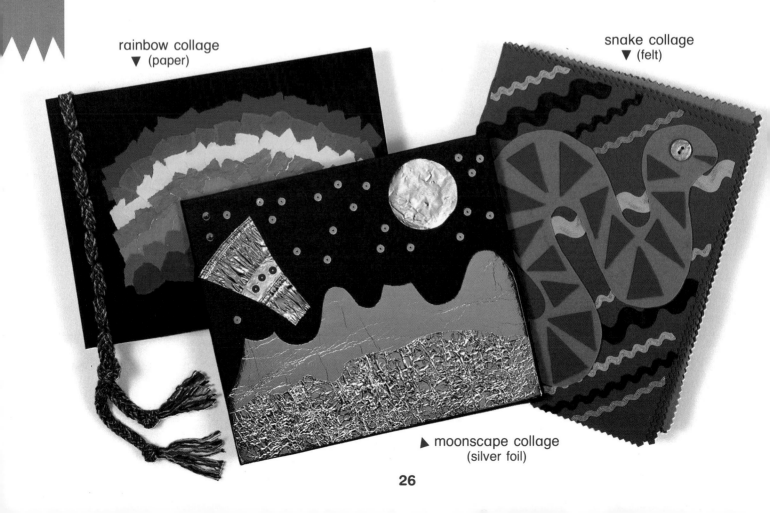

rainbow collage
▼ (paper)

snake collage
▼ (felt)

▲ moonscape collage
(silver foil)

▲ window collage

A Portfolio for your Book Ideas

Making a book may take many weeks. It would be useful to have a simple portfolio to contain all your ideas and artwork.

1. Use two pieces of strong card to make the cover, cut to the size best suited to hold your artwork. Cover the outside of the card with paper—possibly some of your own printed or marbled papers?

2. Cover the inside of both covers with paper cut slightly smaller than the size of the covers.

3. Join the two covers together with strong tape.

4. Cut slits in both covers and thread through a length of ribbon; paste the end to the inside cover.

5. Make flaps for the sides on one of the covers so that your artwork can be tucked inside.

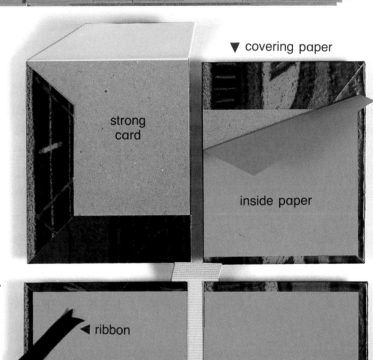

▼ covering paper

strong card

inside paper

◄ ribbon

strong tape ►

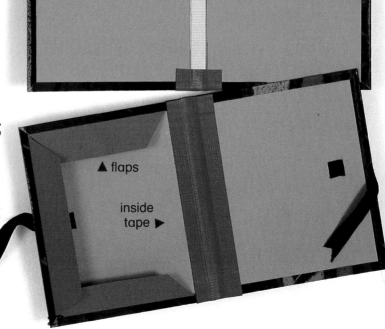

▲ flaps

inside tape ►

Lettering

Words are powerful. Your words are the most important part of your book—through them you communicate with your readers. They must be clear and comfortable to read, but they can still look exciting, dramatic or funny.

Different Ways of Lettering

The main part of your writing will probably be done by hand. If your handwriting is not very clear, help yourself by ruling lines on your pages, or use a stencil. If you are writing your story by hand think about using different coloured pens. If a typewriter or wordprocessor is available use it to achieve a really professional look to your text.

Titles and Headings

You will need larger lettering for your book cover, and possibly for titles and headings inside the book. Use the alphabet on pages 30–31 to get the basic shapes correct. Trace the letters you need and transfer them on to the page for colouring. Alternatively you can cut or tear out letters from coloured paper. For a wider variety of letter shapes look through old magazines and newspapers. Look at some of the examples on this page and try different effects.

Try printing your own letters using a simple potato cut or cardboard block.

How to Trace

1. Fasten tracing paper over your picture using paper-clips, and draw lightly round the image.

2. Remove the tracing paper and shade thickly in pencil over the **back** of the image.

3. Fasten your tracing right side up over your drawing paper, and draw round the image pressing hard.

4. Remove the tracing paper. The image has been transferred to your drawing paper.

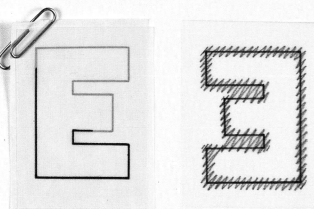

1.　2.

3.

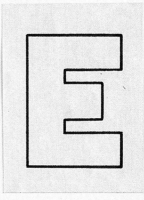

4.

ABCD
HIJ
NOP
UVW

DEFG

KLM

QRST

XYZ

First, you will need to ask an adult to make a paper-making frame. This is made up of two wooden frames of equal size (20 cm × 30 cm). The top frame, called the **deckle**, slots on to the bottom frame and is held in place by hardboard guides. The bottom frame, called the **sieve**, is covered with a fine mesh netting or net curtaining.

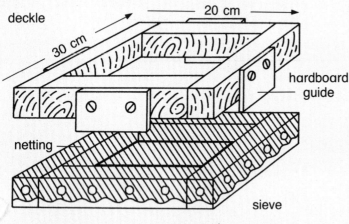

deckle

30 cm

20 cm

hardboard guide

netting

sieve

1. Tear up waste paper and soak overnight in warm water. Photocopier or computer paper is ideal. Add washing-up liquid to help remove any ink.

2. Squeeze out handfuls of the soaked paper and put them into a bowl. Cover with fresh water. Mash to a smooth pulp with your hands or a potato masher. If you wish, colour with food colouring or poster paint. Leave to soak for a few hours.

3. Dip the whole frame into the pulp, shaking it gently to spread the pulp evenly over the netting. Lift out and leave to drain for a minute.

4. Remove the deckle and turn the sieve over carefully on to a J-cloth. The paper is now positioned on the cloth.

5. Wipe the netting with an absorbent cloth to remove as much water as possible. Lift the sieve slowly, leaving your paper on the J-cloth.

6. Lay another J-cloth on top and repeat until all the pulp has been used.

7. Cover the floor with thick layers of newspaper placing the pile of J-cloths and paper in the centre. Put a board on top of the pile and gently stand on it to squeeze out as much water as possible.

8. Remove the board and lay each J-cloth out separately in a warm dry place.

9. While still damp, peel the sheets of paper off the J-cloths and leave them flat to dry completely.